Adventures in Canadian History

BEFORE THE GOLD RUSH

Books for Younger Readers by Pierre Berton

The Golden Trail
The Secret World of Og

ADVENTURES IN CANADIAN HISTORY

The Capture of Detroit
The Death of Isaac Brock
Revenge of the Tribes
Canada Under Siege

Bonanza Gold
The Klondike Stampede
Trails of '98
City of Gold
Before the Gold Rush
Kings of the Klondike

Parry of the Arctic
Jane Franklin's Obsession
Dr. Kane of the Arctic Seas
Trapped in the Arctic

The Railway Pathfinders
The Men in Sheepskin Coats
A Prairie Nightmare
Steel Across the Plains

PIERRE BERTON

The Great Klondike Gold Rush

BEFORE THE GOLD RUSH

ILLUSTRATIONS BY PAUL MC CUSKER

M&S

An M&S Paperback Original from
McClelland & Stewart Inc.
The Canadian Publishers

An M&S Paperback Original from McClelland & Stewart Inc.

First printing October 1993

Canadian Cataloguing in Publication Data

Berton, Pierre, 1920-
Before the gold rush

(Adventures in Canadian history. The great Klondike gold rush)
"An M&S paperback original."
Includes index.
ISBN 0-7710-1449-X

1. Klondike River Valley (Yukon) – Gold discoveries – Juvenile literature.
2. Gold miners – Yukon Territory – Juvenile literature.   I. McCusker, Paul.
II. Title.   III. Series: Berton, Pierre, 1920-   . Adventures in Canadian history. The great Klondike gold rush.

FC4022.3.B477 1993   j971.9'102'0922   C93-094849-1
F1093.B477 1993

Series design by Tania Craan
Cover and text design by Stephen Kenny
Cover illustration by Scott Cameron
Interior illustrations by Paul McCusker
Maps by James Loates
Editor: Peter Carver

Typesetting by M&S, Toronto

The support of the Government of Ontario through the Ministry of Culture, Tourism and Recreation is acknowledged.

Printed and bound in Canada

McClelland & Stewart Inc.
The Canadian Publishers
481 University Avenue
Toronto, Ontario
M5G 2E9

Contents

Map appears on page 8

The events in this book actually happened as told here. Nothing has been made up. This is a work of non-fiction and there is archival evidence for every story and, indeed, every remark made in this book.

Adventures in Canadian History

BEFORE THE GOLD RUSH

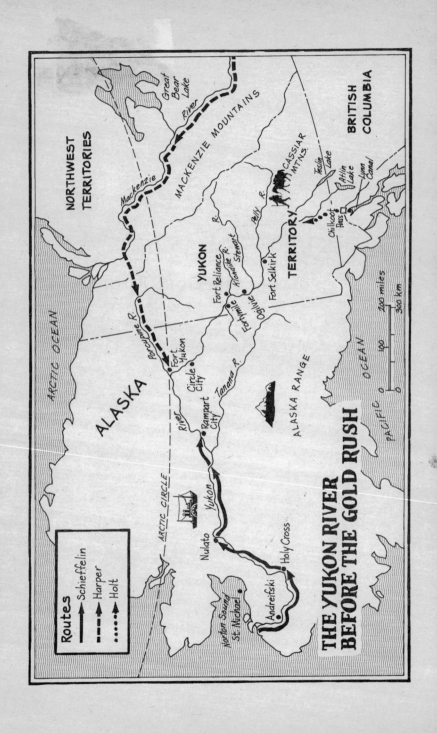

THE YUKON RIVER
BEFORE THE GOLD RUSH

Routes
Schieffelin
Harper
Holt

OVERVIEW

～
The trail of gold

ARTHUR HARPER STUDIED HIS Arrowsmith's map of British North America and asked himself a question: Why should the trail of gold that he had been following since the 1850s stop at British Columbia's northern border?

He was a long-time prospector, an Irishman with a square face, shrewd eyes, and a great beard that would soon turn snow white and give him the look of a frontier patriarch. He was also a veteran of two British Columbia gold rushes, first to the Fraser River in the 1850s, and later to the wide-open Cariboo gold fields in the 1860s.

It seemed to Harper that, if the run of gold stretched from Mexico to British Columbia, it should continue north beyond the horizon.

Beyond the horizon he went, leaving the Cariboo country and pushing down the Peace River in canoes hacked out of cottonwood poplar trunks. With five gallons (22.5 l) of strong rum and five cronies, he followed the line of mountains on their long northward curve across the Arctic Circle and into Alaska.

The author of this book was raised in a house on Harper Street in Dawson. Harper's name and those of other pioneers are still faintly remembered along the Yukon. He was the first of a new breed of adventurer-explorer, tough, honest, hard-working, far-seeing; men who broke trail for the stampede that followed; men who were leaders rather than followers.

Harper and his kind were loners. They lived with solitude and thrived on it. When Arthur Harper started out for the Yukon he had no idea what he would find or where the river would take him. In the civilized world the very name "Yukon" meant nothing. It lay far beyond the mists of the North, vast and totally unknown.

Without men like Harper, the stampede to the goldfields of the Klondike could scarcely have been possible. He was the first of the trailblazers, and it is fitting enough that his name should be on a two-block gravel roadway overlooking the river that was his personal highway. Fitting, yes, but scarcely generous. I lived on Harper Street, but had no idea who Harper was. The schoolbooks I studied did not mention him.

Harper was right about the run of gold. But it did not begin in the mountains of Mexico; it began much farther south. A glittering trail ran up the mountain spine of two continents from the Peruvian Andes to the Bering Sea.

There was gold everywhere in those mountains, and over a period of three centuries, men and women had searched for it – Andean Indians, Spanish *conquistadors,*

American frontiersmen, and ordinary prospectors like Arthur Harper. Much of the history of the New World has been shaped by this search for hidden treasure.

The Indians of the Peruvian Andes were among the first to find it. They learned that gold did not tarnish; it could easily be melted down and reshaped for jewelry, masks, and headpieces. By the time the white men arrived in South America, the successors to those first Indians – the people of the Inca – were rich in gold. That was their downfall.

When the Spanish reached the high Andes, they plundered the Inca gold and killed and enslaved the Indians. They searched far and wide for the fabled City of Gold, the lair of the Golden Man – El Dorado. Somewhere, they believed, it lay hidden in the fastness of the snow-capped peaks. They never found it, but they brought the riches of the Andes back to Spain in galleons loaded with bullion.

The golden trail led north to Mexico and the Sierra Madré in the land of the Aztecs, and then north again to the former Spanish colony of California. It was the search for California's gold that opened the American West. In 1849 thousands of gold-seekers trekked across the empty plains to California. Many moved on north, seeking gold in the streams that ran down the flanks of the Rockies in Colorado and South Dakota. That feverish search spawned Wild West towns with such names as Deadwood and Leadville, and Wild West characters like Wild Bill Hickok.

Again, the trail led north to the colony of British Columbia. In 1857 men like Arthur Harper rushed to the sand bars of the Fraser River to find more gold, and then north again, following the golden highway to the Cariboo country and the boom town of Barkerville. A decade later the lure of gold took them even farther north to the Cassiar Mountains on the very rim of the sub-Arctic.

Beyond that lay the valley of the Yukon, unknown and unexplored. But it would be only a matter of time before more prospectors, following the golden spine of the mountains, burst into the great valleys on the ceaseless search for hidden treasure.

Some found what they were seeking. For all along the 2,200-mile (3,500 km) Yukon River there was gold in great quantities. It was hidden in the bottom of ancient creek beds and in the sands of the smaller river deltas, and even high on the benchland above the valleys that marked the pathway of ancient watercourses.

The gold came from the mountains. Eons before, it had bubbled up out of the ground in molten form when the mountains themselves were created. Now the gold was dust and nuggets. Ceaseless erosion – boulder grating on boulder, gravel grinding against gravel, sand scouring sand – had ground down the original deposits.

That process lasted five million years. The metals that had boiled up through the cracks in the earth's crust were shaved and chiselled away, reduced to muds and clays to be borne off with the current toward the sea. Even the veins of gold that streaked the mountain cores were sandpapered into dust and flour.

Prospector extraordinaire Arthur Harper.

The gold did not reach the sea, for it was too heavy. The finest gold was carried lightly on the crest of mountain torrents until it reached the more leisurely Yukon River, where it sank and was caught in the sand bars at the mouths of the tributary streams.

The coarser gold did not move that distance. As soon as the speed of the current dropped, it was trapped in the crevices of bedrock where nothing could dislodge it.

There it remained over the years, hidden by a blanket of muck growing ever deeper. Thus it lay scattered for the full length of the river – on the hills and in the sand bars, in steep ravines and broad valleys, in underground channels of white gravel, in clefts thirty feet (9 m) beneath the mosses, and in outcroppings poking from the grasses high up on the headland.

There was gold in a dozen tributary rivers that flowed into the Yukon, and in a hundred creeks that flowed into these rivers. This veinwork of running water drained 330,000 miles (528,000 km) of streams, creeks, and rivers, stretching from British Columbia to the Bering Sea. There was gold in Atlin Lake at the very head of the river, and there was gold more than two thousand miles (3,200 km) to the northwest in the sand of the beaches on Norton Sound into which the same river empties.

There was gold everywhere. And where there is gold there are always men to seek it. Long before the beginning of the great stampede which we now know as the Klondike Gold Rush, a trickle of men was coming over the mountains, looking for gold along the river. They could not know that hidden in a small salmon stream, not far from the Alaska-Yukon border, gold lay more thickly than in any other creek, river, or sand bar in the whole of the Yukon. But, with the optimism of the true prospector, each knew that somewhere a vast golden treasure lay hidden. And so they travelled north, each hoping that he would be lucky enough to find it.

CHAPTER ONE

The river

MORE THAN HALF A CENTURY BEFORE the great Klondike stampede, there were whispers of gold somewhere along a mysterious river that led into the dark heart of the great Alaska-Yukon peninsula.

The whispers were little more than murmurs, and they fell at first on Russian ears, for the Russians then owned Alaska. Russian traders had reached the mouth of the great river, which the Loucheaux Indians called "Yukon," or "*Yukunn-ah*" (Great River), in 1834; but they didn't care about gold any more than did the native peoples who lived along the river's banks, fishing for salmon.

But the whispers were heard in Sitka, the Russian capital of Alaska, situated on an island in the Pacific along that strip of coastal land known as the Panhandle. This was the headquarters of Alexander Baranov, known as the Lord of Alaska, who had been sent by the Czars to gather a fortune in furs to enrich the imperial family. In these godforsaken surroundings, Baranov managed to live like a prince –

surrounded by fine books, costly paintings, and brilliantly costumed officers and women.

Baranov was after seals, not gold. To his Russian-American fur company they represented a true fortune. The last thing he wanted was a gold rush – a horde of tough American and British prospectors trampling into Russian territory and ruining his monopoly. When one of the Russians babbled drunkenly of gold, Baranov, so legend has it, ordered him shot.

When the traders of the Hudson's Bay Company entered the Yukon valley in the 1840s, they too heard whispers of gold along the river. They built two trading posts on the Yukon. The first – Fort Yukon – was situated at the mouth of the Porcupine, where the great river makes its majestic curve over the Arctic Circle. Then they built a second – Fort Selkirk – some six hundred miles (960 km) upstream, at the point where the Yukon is joined by the muddy Pelly.

This was unmapped, unexplored land. Nobody had yet travelled the full length of the great water highway. The Hudson's Bay traders knew so little about the geography that they didn't realize both forts were on the same river.

Nor did they realize that Fort Yukon was actually deep in Russian territory. They were far from civilization; their crude maps were inaccurate; and nobody could be sure exactly where the boundary was that divided Russian Alaska from British North America.

They had heard whispers of gold, but they took no

action. Robert Campbell, the chief trader at Fort Selkirk, actually found traces of it. He wasn't the least interested. Like Baranov, he felt that furs were the real treasure.

We know that another Hudson's Bay clerk wrote home to Toronto reporting that an Anglican missionary, Archdeacon McDonald, had seen so much gold in a small river not far away that he could have gathered it in a spoon. But the minister was not interested in gold either. His task was to translate prayer books for the Loucheaux. As for the clerk, he wrote that he had "often wished to go but can never find the time." Perhaps he was lucky that the gold fever, which destroyed so many men, passed him by.

In 1867, the year of Canadian Confederation, the United States bought Alaska from the Russians. The Americans drove the Hudson's Bay Company out of Fort Yukon and the Chilkoot Indians, a warlike band, came in from the ocean and drove the company out of Fort Selkirk.

But there were still wanderers who had a burning desire to seek gold. The new territory of Alaska was both a land to conquer and also a wilderness to which a man could flee. The territory was shaped like a kitchen pot – a long strip of coastal land, the Panhandle, was attached to the main body of the Alaska Peninsula, bordering on the Pacific territories of British Columbia. In 1880, at a point midway down this panhandle, hardrock gold was discovered and the mining town of Juneau sprang up.

There are two kinds of gold in the Northwest. Hardrock gold is discovered in veins hidden in the mountains. It must be blasted free from tunnels driven deep into the rock. To get at this gold, a lucky prospector had to raise large sums of money to form a company to buy the expensive equipment needed to mine the veins.

"Placer gold," or "free gold," was created by the erosion of the centuries. Ground into nuggets and dust by wind and water, it is found deep beneath the soil in the bedrock of ancient watercourses. A single man, if he is industrious enough, can find and mine this gold by sinking a shaft, hauling up the "pay dirt," and sluicing the lighter clays and sands away, leaving the gold behind.

Juneau served as a springboard to the interior Yukon valley. In 1880, when gold was discovered there, the wanderers and adventurers, the Indian-fighters and the frontiersmen of the American West – men who could not sit still – headed north.

These prospectors were men who had spent most of their lives seeking gold. They'd come up through Arizona, Colorado, Nevada, and Idaho, leaving behind names like Virginia City, Cripple Creek, and Tombstone. They had moved up the wrinkled hide of British Columbia, through the sombre canyons of the Fraser and the rolling grasslands of the Cariboo to the snowfields of the Cassiars.

They came at first in twos and threes and they carried little more than a rucksack, a gold pan, a short-stemmed shovel, and a vial of mercury to separate the gold from the lesser sands. They lived on beans and tea and bacon. Most were men fleeing ahead of civilization. Whenever they struck it rich, a circus of camp-followers crowded in behind them – saloon-keepers, dance-hall girls, gamblers, vigilantes, and tenderfeet.

And so, as the horde grew larger and the pioneers moved farther north, valleys became industrial bees' nests and meadows were transformed into brawling shack towns. The sighing of the wind and the roaring of the river were drowned by the tuneless scraping of dance-hall violins and the crash of butchered timber.

Finally, like the forward patrols of a mighty army, the first prospectors reached the last frontier. In the 1870s and 1880s they began to move into the Yukon valley.

The Yukon is the fifth largest river in North America. Unlike most great watercourses, it begins just fifteen miles (24 km) from the saltwater of the Pacific Ocean on the eastern side of the great coastal mountain wall, and then travels on a 2,200-mile (3,500 km) search for that same saltwater. That search takes it on a winding journey across the face of Alaska and the Yukon.

It rises as a trickle in the mountain snowfields that feed the green alpine lakes. From there it pushes incessantly through barriers of rock flowing to the northwest, until it crosses the Arctic Circle. There it falters as if unsure of itself and hesitates on the Circle's edge, only to change its mind and turn in its tracks. Now it doubles back, plunging southwestward, defying every obstacle until it spreads itself wide in a mighty delta to pour into the cold waters of Norton Sound across from the easternmost tip of Siberia.

This awkward, roundabout route is the result of the odd tilting of the interior plateau. But without that long and aimless coil of the great river, there would be no water highway into the heart of the Northwest.

As with the river, so with the men who sought the gold. They too arrived by roundabout routes. They too often moved hesitantly. And like the river whose quest for saltwater seems futile, their quest for gold brought early disappointment. Yet in the end, like the river, some of them found what they were seeking.

CHAPTER TWO

The pioneers

THE FIRST PROSPECTORS ENTERED THE great Alaska-Yukon peninsula from three different directions. Three are famous because they were the first.

In 1873, as we have seen, Arthur Harper entered from northern Canada. He had travelled in a roundabout route north and west from the Peace and the Mackenzie river valleys in a wide arc before he reached his goal.

In 1878 George Holt took the shortest route. He came directly in from the seacoast, having climbed the Chilkoot Pass, which at the time was the only known gap in the mountains that screened off the interior plateau from the sea.

In 1882 Ed Schieffelin took the water route by boat, all the way around to the Bering Sea opposite Siberia. He built a second boat – a tiny, stern-wheeled steamboat – and moved up the long water highway of the Yukon River itself.

Harper's name is still remembered in the Yukon. He was, after all, the first white prospector to enter the Yukon valley. For two thousand miles (3,200 km) he and his party had paddled and prospected the creeks on both sides of the great divide that separates the Yukon from the valley of the Mackenzie. It was a backbreaking adventure. They were forced to drag their boats over mountain divides and haul them through the shallow waters of frothing streams – their feet half frozen, their limbs ulcerated from the wet and the cold. But they found nothing.

At last they reached the Yukon River at the point where it coils across the Arctic Circle. For the next quarter of a century the river was Harper's highway – and he had it all to himself. He roamed it ceaselessly, seeking gold in every stream, testing the gravels and panning the sand bars, always hoping to find the treasure, yet never succeeding.

We know now that the gold was under his nose, but he missed it. He explored four rivers that later yielded fortunes – the Stewart, the Fortymile, the Tanana, and the Klondike. But he didn't make the longed-for discovery.

By the time the gold was discovered and the stampede had begun, it was too late for Arthur Harper. Suffering from tuberculosis, he headed back to the sunlit valleys of Arizona and there, at the height of the gold rush, he died. A street in Dawson City bears his name.

George Holt didn't find any gold either. Now a vague and shadowy figure, scarcely more than a name in the early history of Alaska, he is remembered for a remarkable feat. He was the first white man to get through the massive wall of angry peaks that seals off the Yukon valley from the North Pacific. These mountains were guarded by three thousand natives and no one knows how he got past them.

In this mountain wall a tiny notch had been ripped out by the shrieking winds. It could be reached only after a thousand-foot (350 m) climb up a thirty-five degree slope that was strewn with immense boulders. For eight months out of twelve, it was caked with solid ice. Glaciers of bottle green overhung it like huge icicles ready to burst at the end of summer. Avalanches thundered down from the mountains in the spring. In the winter the snow fell so thickly it could reach a depth of seventy feet (21 m). This forbidding gap was called the Chilkoot Pass. Holt was the first white man to see it. Twenty years later thousands would climb it – over and over again – in a new search for gold.

This was the gateway to the unknown Yukon valley, but the Chilkoot Indians guarded it jealously. These were men of immense strength, squat, sturdy, and heavy-shouldered, able to lug a two-hundred-pound (90 kg) pack across the mountains without a rest. They controlled all the trade with the Han Indians of the interior – a people whom they dominated. It was these Chilkoots who had driven the powerful Hudson's Bay Company from Fort Selkirk back in 1852.

Somehow – we don't know how – Holt got past this human obstacle. He scaled the pass and emerged into that dark land where the Yukon has its beginning. In 1878 he came out with two small nuggets that an Indian from Alaska had given him.

Holt's stories of gold, much of it the result of his own

George Holt reaches the summit of the Chilkoot Pass.

active imagination, excited the interest of newcomers at Sitka. By this time the old Russian capital was teeming with gold-seekers who had originally come north to seek their fortune in the Cassiar Mountains of British Columbia. Now Holt had suggested new fields to conquer. And so twenty prospectors, protected by a U.S. gunboat, headed for the foot of the mountains. There they fired a few blank rounds from a Gatling gun, enough to convince the Indians that the pass should be opened.

In this way the dam was broken. From 1880 onward, a trickle of men began to cross the divide. The Indians didn't suffer. They charged a fee to pack the white men's outfits over the mountains and, being clever traders, they always got what the traffic would bear. By the time of the Klondike Stampede, they had raised the price to a dollar a pound (145 kg). Thus, without ever sinking a pan into the creekbeds of the Yukon, the Chilkoots grew rich.

George Holt, having got past one barrier, now tried to get past another. He moved west to wilder land to invade the copper country of the Chettyna in southern Alaska. The Indians there had no intention of letting him through. They had already killed three men. Poor Holt made the fourth.

By this time some of the prospectors who had followed Holt into the Yukon interior were beginning to find flour gold in the sand bars of the Yukon. Flour gold is just what it sounds like – gold that has been ground into a dust so delicate that it can almost float on the surface of the water.

Placer gold is moved downstream by the force of the rushing water. The coarser gold soon sinks and is caught in the crevices of the bedrock, but the power of the water continues to move the finer gold. By the time a creek enters the Yukon River, only the finest gold – the flour gold – is left to settle into the sand bars at the mouth.

It was not easy to separate this very fine gold from the sands that surrounded it, but some prospectors succeeded. Rumours of their finds began to filter down through the Rocky Mountain mining camps of the western United States. By 1882 these stories reached the ears of a gaunt scarecrow of a prospector named Ed Schieffelin.

This was no penniless gold-seeker. In the Apache country of Arizona, Schieffelin had discovered a mountain of silver and founded the town of Tombstone. This was the same community in which Wyatt Earp and the Clanton Brothers would soon shoot it out at the O.K. Corral.

Schieffelin was worth a million dollars, but he didn't look like a millionaire. His beard and his glossy black hair hung long in ringlets, and his grey, ghost-eyes had the faraway look of a long-time prospector.

He had been a prospector all his life, panning gold as a child in Oregon and running off at the age of twelve to join a gold stampede. In the generation that followed, he was in almost every boom camp in the West. He didn't need to lock for treasure, but the fever was in him. He wanted to repeat his success in Alaska.

Like Harper, Schieffelin had studied the maps and

arrived at an odd theory. He believed that a great mineral belt girdled the world from Cape Horn to Asia and down through the western mountains of North America to the Andes. As we know, he was partially right. Somewhere in Alaska, he thought, the golden highway ought to cross the Yukon valley. He meant to find it.

And so, in the spring of 1883, he and his small party arrived at St. Michael, the old Russian port on the Bering Sea just to the north of the Yukon's mouth. There he built his tiny steamboat, the *New Racket,* and set off up the unexplored river.

See him now, puffing slowly around the coast of Norton Sound and into the maze of the great Yukon delta where the channels fan out for sixty-five miles (104 km), where the banks are grey with silt and where long-legged cranes stalk the marshes.

Here were islands that had never been counted. Here a man could lose himself forever in half a hundred twisting channels. At this point Schieffelin was more than two thousand miles (3,200 km) from the Chilkoot Pass, which Holt had crossed five years before. Before him lay the unknown.

The little boat chugged out into the river proper. This was a land with terraced valleys, sleeping glaciers, and high clay banks pocked by swallows' nests and bright with brier rose and bluebell – an empty land of legend and mystery. So little was known about it that, in London, globes of the world were still being issued showing the Yukon River flowing north into the Arctic Ocean instead of west into the Bering Sea.

Many stories were told and believed of this mysterious country – stories of prehistoric mammoths who roamed the hills with jets of live steam issuing from their nostrils, and of the immense bears that prowled the mountain peaks in endless circles, because their limbs were longer on one side than on the other.

To Schieffelin, the broad Yukon seemed endless. It wound on and on, tawny and cold, gnawing through walls of granite and wriggling past mountain ranges, spilling out over miles of flatland at one point, squeezed between black pillars of rock at another.

Once in a while tiny pinpoints of civilization broke the monotony of the grey-green forest land – deserted Russian missions and Indian graves on the high bank above. For a thousand miles (1,600 km), the little steamer struggled against the current, working its way deeper and deeper into unexplored country – past Burning Mountain, a smoking seam of coal; past the Palisades, cliff-like castles of rock that guarded the mouth of the Tanana River; and finally into the brooding hills known as the Lower Ramparts, where the river channels are gathered into a single rustling gorge.

Here, poking among the mosses on the rock, Ed Schieffelin found some specks of gold, and he was convinced he had stumbled upon the mineral belt he believed encircled the earth. But there was frost in the air and

Schieffelin was accustomed to the fierce Arizona sun. The bleakness of the Arctic summer had already discouraged him. He decided that mining could never pay along the Yukon.

Back he went, without exploring the rest of the river that drifted for another thousand miles to gateway of the Chilkoot. And so, as it had eluded Harper and Holt, the gold of the Yukon eluded the gaunt Schieffelin.

For the rest of his life he would never cease to prospect. In fact he was still seeking a new mine when he died of a heart attack in front of his cabin in the forests of Oregon. The year was 1897, and the world was buzzing with tales of a fortune to be found in the land he had dismissed as frozen waste.

CHAPTER THREE

The traders

FOR FIVE YEARS AFTER SCHIEFFELIN left the Yukon, nothing happened.

The land remained silent and empty. Small groups of prospectors continued to dribble over the Chilkoot Pass to test the sand bars along the headwaters. But for eighteen hundred miles (2,880 km), the river was almost untravelled. The only boats on its surface were those of the natives and of the occasional trader working on a commission for the Alaska Commercial Company, the descendant of the old Russian-American Fur Company.

That's how Arthur Harper scratched out a living. Unable to find a fortune in the shifting sands of the little creeks, Harper had taken to trading tea and flour in return for furs that he trapped along the river. But Harper is remembered in the Yukon to this day because he opened up the Yukon valley to those who followed seeking gold.

Two men joined him. They were a strange pair. One was a lean, wiry little thong of a man, the other a six-foot giant with a barrel chest.

The little man's name was Al Mayo. There is a town named after him in the Yukon. He was a one-time circus acrobat driven north by wanderlust, given to practical jokes, and blessed with a dry wit. He used to claim in his later years that he had been in the country so long that when he first arrived, the Yukon River was a small creek and the Chilkoot Pass a hole in the ground.

The big man's name was LeRoy Napoleon McQuesten, but everybody called him plain "Jack." A ruddy man with a flowing blond moustache, he had all the restlessness of his breed. He had been a farmer in Maine, an Indian-fighter in the West, and a gold-hunter on the Fraser River.

Just as Harper was a frustrated prospector, McQuesten was a frustrated voyageur. He had one fierce ambition: he wanted so badly to become a voyageur that he gave himself a course in physical training. He would need that if he was going to perform the incredible feats of strength and endurance for which the early voyageurs were noted.

He signed on with the Hudson's Bay Company in the Athabasca country, only to discover, to his disappointment, that he could not handle the crushing two-hundred-pound (90 kg) loads that his French-Canadian companions hoisted so easily on their backs. So he drifted across the mountains into the Yukon valley, and there he met Harper and Mayo.

The three men became partners. For more than fifteen years they were alone in the land. The river was their private highway. They could drift down it for a thousand miles

(1,600 km) without seeing another white face. In fact, McQuesten once recalled he'd gone six years without tasting flour.

They all took Indian wives, but they did not resemble the so-called "squaw men" who were looked down upon by their fellows. Their wives and families lived in handsome homes with square-cut logs and with neat vegetable gardens at the rear. The wives were partners in a true sense. The children were sent out to be educated in private schools in the United States. Years later, when McQuesten retired, he took his Indian wife to California where she ran the big family home in Berkeley. When he died she managed his estate and continued as the head of the family.

The country changed these three. They had been restless and temperamental. But over the long decades they had developed a serenity that became the envy of those who met them. Frederick Schwatka, a U.S. cavalry officer who was the first man to explore the Yukon River for its full length, came upon McQuesten in 1883. He watched in admiration as the trader bargained for hours with Indians, unruffled by the endless discussions that Schwatka said "would have put Job in a frenzy."

McQuesten, Mayo, and Harper never presented a bill, yet they were seldom short-changed. Once, when a cargo of goods arrived, and a group of miners became impatient for provisions, Harper told them simply to help themselves, keep their own accounts, and hand them in at their leisure. The only missing item was six cans of condensed milk.

They built their first post at Fort Reliance, only a few miles from the mouth of the Thron-diuck, or Klondike, River. It became the focus for future river settlements. Several neighbouring rivers took their names from the distance that separated them from that post. Thus, the Fortymile and the Twelvemile rivers were named because they joined the Yukon that distance downstream from Fort Reliance. The Sixtymile was so called because it was sixty miles (96 km) upstream from the fort. Later on, the towns established at the mouths of these rivers took the same names.

It is ironic that this first river settlement should have been so close to the stream that came to be called Klondike – strange because, though they hunted and prospected along its valley, none of the partners was destined to grow wealthy on Klondike gold. They had come into the country to look for gold, but now they were traders, and gold no longer excited them.

Perhaps this was just as well. Most of those who chased gold in the Klondike in the years that followed died in poverty. But when the madness struck, these three kept their heads. When they died it was with the respect of everyone who had known them.

In the words of one Alaska Commercial Company employee, they were "typically frontiersmen, absolutely honest, without a semblance of fear of anything, and to a great extent childlike in their implicit faith in human nature, looking on their fellow pioneers as being equally as honest as themselves." This could not have been said of many who came later.

These men, and a fourth named Joseph Ladue, who arrived a decade later, were the true pioneers and true founders of both the Yukon Territory of Canada and the U.S. State of Alaska. Without their presence the series of events that led to the great Klondike discovery would not have been possible. Without the string of posts they set up along the Yukon, the early exploration of the river country could not have taken place.

It was they who guided the hands of the prospectors. It was they who outfitted them without demanding instant cash – and sent them off to promising sections of the country. They followed up each discovery by laying out a townsite and erecting and building a general store.

Their little steamboat, the *New Racket,* which they had bought from Schieffelin, was their lifeline to the outside world. They made a casual arrangement with the great Alaska Commercial Company in San Francisco. In the early years they were on its payroll, but they remained free to prospect if they wished. Later they operated as independent contractors, buying their goods from the company but trading on their own.

Sometimes they worked together as partners, sometimes separately. There were other traders scattered along the river working with similar arrangements with the company. But it was these men, far more than the others, who were

Al Mayo and Jack McQuesten and the New Racket.

responsible for the mining development in the Yukon and the first of the famous mining camps.

It is not always realized that a series of smaller gold rushes into the Yukon valley took place before the great Klondike stampede. In fact, Dawson City was preceded by several mining camps that sprang up along the river in the decade before the great strike. Since all the gold along the Yukon was placer gold – the kind that could be mined by any man with a shovel and a pan and a strong back – it was attractive to the penniless men who made their way north from the civilized world.

By 1886 there were about two hundred miners working their way for three hundred miles (480 km) down the Yukon, from the Chilkoot Pass to the mouth of the Stewart River. In a single year these men panned out one hundred thousand dollars' worth of fine gold from the sand bars, a sum equal to at least a million today.

McQuesten and his partners built a trading post at the Stewart, suspecting that the human flow would increase. But McQuesten was worried. There wasn't enough food in all of the Yukon to feed the men who would be attracted to the Stewart. He decided to go to San Francisco to order more supplies and equipment from the Alaska Commercial Company.

That winter Arthur Harper persuaded two prospectors to try the waters of the Fortymile River, which joined the Yukon another hundred miles (160 km) farther downstream. Here they found the gold that had eluded Harper –

good coarse gold that rattled in the pan, the kind that every miner seeks. At once the men along the Stewart deserted their diggings and flocked to the new strike.

Harper was in a panic. He knew what was coming. As soon as the news leaked back up the river and across the mountain barrier to the outside world, hundreds of men would tumble over the peaks and pour down to the new diggings on the crest of the spring torrents. There certainly wasn't food enough in the land to supply this horde. Harper knew he must get word of the new strike out to McQuesten to increase his order. Otherwise there would be starvation along the Yukon.

He felt like a man in a soundproof prison. To all intents, the interior of the Northwest was sealed off from the world by winter. It was virtually impossible to get Outside. He might as well be living on the moon.

The nearest point of civilization was John Healy's trading post on Dyea Inlet on the far side of the Chilkoot. But in between lay an untravelled wilderness – a jungle of forest, rock, snow, and mountains. Few men had ever made it in the winter. Who would carry Harper's message?

Of all people, a steamboat man named Tom Williams volunteered. He had no experience in "mushing," as the pioneers called it. But he went anyway with one Indian companion on a terrifying journey.

The two men plunged for five hundred miles (800 km) over the hummocks of river ice and the corpses of fallen trees, through the cold tangle of the Yukon forest and up the slippery flanks of the mountains. By the time they reached the Chilkoot their rations were gone and their dogs dead of cold, hunger, and fatigue.

When they reached the top of the pass, a blizzard was raging. Travel became impossible. They clawed a cave out of the snow and crouched in it, their fingers, faces, and feet blackened by frostbite. Their food was gone. They only had a few mouthfuls of dry flour left to keep them alive.

When the flour ran out, the Indian hoisted the exhausted Williams onto his back and stumbled down the slope of the pass until he could carry him no farther. He dropped him into the snow and staggered on until he reached Sheep Camp – a long-time stopping point on the edge of the tree line. We do not know the name of this enterprising native – nor his history. Nobody bothered to set it down, for in those days, the Indians were seen as faceless creatures of the forest – like the caribou or the black bears.

It was now March of 1887. A group of prospectors camped in the shelter of the mountains, hoping for the storm to subside, watched in astonishment as the figure of the Indian loomed out of the swirling snow. They followed him back up the mountain and helped to bring Williams down to Sheep Camp, where they revived him with hot soup.

The Indian borrowed a sled and dragged his companion twenty-six miles (42 km) down the trail to Dyea Inlet. Here, the two men finally reached the shelter of the trading

Carrying Tom Williams down the Chilkoot.

post run by the one-time Montana sheriff named John J. Healy. Williams lived for two days, and the men who crowded around his deathbed had only one question: Why on earth had he made the trip?

It was the Indian's answer that electrified them. He reached into a sack of beans on Healy's counter and flung a handful onto the floor.

"Gold," he said. "All same like this!"

CHAPTER FOUR

A community of hermits

ALONG THE HIGH BANK AT THE POINT where the Fortymile River joins the Yukon – on the very edge of the Alaska-Yukon border – a weird and lonely Canadian village straggled into being as a result of Tom Williams' dying message.

This was Fortymile, named for the river that flowed into the Yukon about forty miles (64 km) downstream from Fort Reliance. It's hard for us to understand today how far it was from civilization.

For eight months out of twelve, its residents lived as if in a vacuum, sealed off from the world. The nearest outfitting port was San Francisco – almost five thousand water miles (8,000 km) away. The only links with the sea were two tiny stern-wheelers: the *New Racket,* owned by Harper and his partners, and the Alaska Commercial Company's *Arctic,* built in 1889.

There was only time for these boats to attempt one summer trip upstream from the old Russian seaport of St.

Michael, not far from the river's mouth on the Bering Sea. And sometimes even that wasn't time enough.

On her first voyage, the *Arctic* was damaged and could not bring supplies to Fortymile. The company sent Indian runners sixteen hundred miles (2,560 km) upriver to the settlement to warn the miners that they faced starvation. With no supplies arriving from the outside world they would have to escape from the Yukon valley.

As the October snows drifted down from the dark skies, the residents of Fortymile pressed aboard the little *New Racket*. The tiny vessel made a brave attempt to reach St. Michael before the river froze, but she was caught in the ice floes one hundred and ninety miles (304 km) short of her goal. The starving passengers had to trudge the rest of the way on foot. Those who stayed behind in Fortymile spent a hungry winter. One man, in fact, lived for nine months on a steady diet of flapjacks.

The only winter route to the outside world was the dreadful trek upstream to the Chilkoot – more than six hundred miles (960 km) away. After Williams' death very few people had the courage to try it. Four men did attempt it in 1893, but they were forced to leave fifteen thousand dollars' worth of gold dust on the mountain slopes. They were so badly crippled by the shrieking winds and the intense cold that one died and another was disabled for life.

Why would anyone want to wall himself off from the

world in a village of logs deep in the sub-Arctic wilderness? Who were they?

In one sense they were men chasing a fortune – chasing it with such passion that it had brought them to the ends of the earth. But there was more to it than that. They seemed more like men pursued than men pursuing. The truth is that if they searched for anything it was the right to be left alone.

Father William Judge, a Jesuit missionary in Alaska, described them as "men running away from civilization as it advanced westward – until they'd have no farther to go and so have to stop." Judge met one man who had been born in the United States so long ago that he had never seen a railway. He'd kept moving on ahead of the rails until he reached the banks of the Yukon.

There were veterans of the American Civil War in Fortymile and old Indian-fighters. There were younger sons, black sheep many of them, sent out from England with a bit of money to keep them away – people called them "remittance men." There were prospectors from the far west, many of whom had known each other in the various camps in the Black Hills of Idaho and in Colorado.

They were all nomads, stirred by a wanderlust that seized them at the slightest whisper of a new strike, no matter how flimsy the rumours were. Their natures were such that they each craved the widest possible freedom of action. And yet each was also disciplined by a code of friendship whose unwritten rules were as strict as any law.

Three prospectors and their tame moose.

Their nicknames, which were far commoner than real names, suggested that none of them was cut from the same cloth. Salt Water Jack, Big Dick, Squaw Cameron, Jimmy the Pirate, Muckskin Miller, Pete the Pig – that was how they were known. In the civilized world they would have been thought of as very strange.

One man, known as the Old Maiden, carried fifty pounds (23 kg) of old newspapers about with him wherever he went. He said they were "handy to refer to when you get into an argument." Another was dubbed Cannibal Ike because he used to hack off great slabs of moose meat with his knife and stuff them raw into his mouth.

One cabin at Fortymile had walls almost as thin as paper because the owner kept chopping away at the logs to feed his fire. He said he did it to let in the light. In another cabin were three partners and a tame moose, which they treated as a house pet. Out on the river, on Liar's Island, a group of exiles whiled away the long winters telling tales that nobody really believed.

This strange little village of log cabins, at the point where the Fortymile River joins the Yukon, was a community of hermits. If the residents had one thing in common, it was the desire to be left alone.

"I feel so long dead and buried that I cannot think a short visit home, as from the grave, would be of much use," wrote William Bompas, a Church of England bishop who was stationed at Fortymile. Bompas was a Cambridge graduate who could read his Bible in Greek, Hebrew, and Syriac. He was the fourth son of a London lawyer.

The clergyman who preceded him had been driven mad by the practical jokes of the miners, but Bompas was too tough for that. He was a giant with a huge dome, hawk-nose, piercing eyes, and a flowing beard. He baked his own bread, drank his sugarless coffee from an iron cup, ate from a tin plate with a knife his only utensil, slept in the corner of a boat or in a hole in the snow or on the floor of a log hut.

He took no holidays. His only furniture was a box he used for a seat. He had torn down the shelves and cupboards to make a coffin for a dead native, because lumber was so scarce. He thought nothing of making a present of his trousers to an unfortunate Indian who had no pants. The tough bishop mushed all the way home wearing only his red flannel underwear.

He had lived in isolation and was resigned to it. His wife was the daughter of a fashionable London doctor, and had been brought up in Italy. When she finally joined him in 1892, they hadn't seen each other for five years. On those dark winter afternoons when she wasn't out on the trail with her husband, she sat quietly in the mission hall with its cotton-drill walls, reading the Italian poet Dante in the original Italian, or playing on her little harmonium – that is, if the the keys weren't frozen stiff.

Yet this frontier way of life was no more primitive than that of the others. Each miner lived with his partner in a murky, airless cabin whose windowpanes were made from untanned deerhide, white cotton canvas, or a row of empty pickle jars chinked with moss. Knives and forks were made of pieces of tin. Furniture was built from the stumps of trees. Four men often lived year in and year out in a space no more than eighteen feet (5.5 m) square.

Hanging above the red-hot sheet-iron stove, there was always a tin of fermented dough. It was used in place of yeast to make biscuits, bread, and flapjacks rise. That was the origin of the name "sourdough," which was applied to the pioneers in the Yukon to distinguish them from the newcomers – the tenderfeet or *cheechakos*.

Every morning the men left their cabins to crawl into the murky, constricted mine shafts. The mining in the sub-Arctic was unlike mining anywhere else in the world. For here the ground was permanently frozen and had to be thawed before the bedrock, which contained the gold, could be reached. This bedrock lay ten or twenty feet (3 to 6 m) below the surface.

To reach bedrock, the first miners let the sun do the work. That was a tedious, backbreaking process. Each day a few inches of thawed earth were scraped away. Each day the shaft in the permafrost grew a few inches deeper. An entire summer might pass before bedrock was reached.

Later on, wood fires replaced the sun. The gold-seekers lit them by night, removing the ashes and thawed earth each morning. The fires burned their way slowly down to form a shaft whose sides remained frozen as hard as granite.

The new method allowed miners to work all winter, choking and wheezing in smoky, ice-sheathed dungeons, far below the snowy surface of the ground. When they reached bedrock they tunnelled this way and that, seeking the "pay streak" that marked an old creek channel. When they hit pay dirt, they hoisted it up the shaft with a windlass and a pail and piled it in a mound they called a "dump."

In the spring, when the ice broke in the creeks and water gushed down the hillsides, the miners built long spillways, or "sluice boxes," to copy the ancient action of nature. Gravel containing the pay dirt was shovelled into these boxes. As the water rushed through the gravel and sand it was swept away by force of the tide. The gold, being nineteen times as heavy as water, was caught in the cross bars and in matting lying on the bottom. This is exactly what had happened in the creeks eons before, when the gold was caught in the crevices of the bedrock before the ancient streambeds were covered by an overlay of muck.

Every two or three days, the water was diverted from the sluice box, and then each miner panned the residue at the bottom in what became known as a "clean-up."

The entertainments that lightened this monotony were rare and primitive. One of the main amusements was a folk-rite known in the slang of the day as a "squaw dance." Josiah Edward Spurr, a U.S. government geologist who visited Fortymile in the old days, has left a description of one of these affairs.

"We were attracted by a row of miners who were lined up

in front of the saloon engaged in watching the door of a very large log cabin opposite, rather dilapidated with the windows broken in…. They said there was going to be a dance, but when or how they did not seem to know….

"The evening wore on until ten o'clock, when in the dusk a stolid Indian woman with a baby in the blanket on her back, came cautiously around the corner, and with the peculiar long slouchy step of her kind, made for the cabin door, looking neither to the right nor to the left….

A dance at Fortymile.

"She was followed by a dozen others, one far behind another, each silent and unconcerned, and each with a baby upon her back. They sidled into the log cabin and sat down on the benches, where they also deposited their babies in a row: the little red people lay there very still, with wide eyes shut or staring, but never crying....

"The mothers sat awhile looking at the ground on some one spot, then slowly lifted their heads to look at the miners who had slouched into the cabin after them – men fresh

from the diggings, spoiling for excitement of any kind. Then a man with a dilapidated fiddle struck up a swinging, sawing melody and in the intoxication of the moment some of the most reckless of the miners grabbed an Indian woman and began furiously swinging her around in a sort of waltz while the others crowded and looked on.

"Little by little the dusk grew deeper, but candles were scarce and could not be afforded. The figures of the dancing couples grew more and more indistinct and their faces became lost to view, while the sawing of the fiddle grew more and more rapid, and the dancing more excited. There was no noise, however; scarcely a sound save the fiddle and the shuffling of the feet over the floor of rough hewn logs; for the Indian women were as stolid as ever and the miners could not speak the language of their partners. Even the lookers on said nothing, so that these silent dancing figures in the dusk made an almost weird effect.

"One by one, however, the women dropped out, tired, picked up their babies and slouched off home, and the men slipped over to the saloon to have a drink before going to their cabins. Surely this squawdance, as they call it, was one of the most peculiar balls ever seen...."

CHAPTER FIVE

The Mounties bring order

As the years passed, a thin varnish of civilization began to spread over Fortymile. Some saloons had Chippendale chairs. Some stores even sold *pâté de foie gras,* tinned plum pudding, and other delicacies. Shakespeare clubs were formed to give play readings. A library opened; its shelves contained books on science and philosophy. A dressmaker arrived to fill the latest Paris fashions. An opera house was opened with a troupe of San Francisco dance-hall girls. There was even a cigar factory.

All these institutions were housed in log buildings strewn helter-skelter along the muddy bank above the Yukon and surrounded by a marshland that was littered with stumps, wood shavings, and tin cans.

There were ten saloons in Fortymile, around which the social life of the camp revolved. At steamboat time, the saloons served whisky at fifty cents a drink – heavily watered to make it last. For the rest of the year they peddled hootchinoo, a vile mixture of molasses, sugar, and dried fruit, fermented with sourdough, flavoured with anything handy, distilled in an empty coal-oil can, and sometimes served hot, at fifty cents a drink. Hootchinoo was sometimes known as Forty-Rod Whisky because it was supposed to kill a man at that distance. (A rod is about 5 m.)

There were strict unwritten rules in the saloons. For instance, a man who bought a drink had to buy for everybody in the house, even though the round might cost a hundred dollars. It was a deadly insult to refuse a drink under these circumstances, but a teetotaller could accept a fifty-cent cigar in its place.

Like everything else, hootch was paid for in gold dust. The prospector who flung his poke of dust on the bar always performed a gesture of turning his back while the amount was weighed out. To watch the weighing was to suggest that the bartender was crooked.

Fortymile thrived on these unwritten rules. It might be said that the community was run informally. There was no mayor or council. There were no judges or lawyers. There was no police, no jail, no written laws.

Yet the people stuck together. Nobody went hungry, though many were broke. Credit at Harper and McQuesten's store was unlimited. If a man had no money, he could still get an outfit without paying.

There were very few "bad men" in Fortymile. In a way it was more of a Christian community than many towns in the outside world. Men shared their good fortune with their comrades. It was part of the code that he who struck a new creek spread the news to everybody. Each man's cabin was open to any passerby. The traveller could enter, eat what he needed, sleep in the absent owner's bed, and then go on his way. But he must clean up before he left and he must leave a fresh supply of kindling. That was important. For this was a country in which a freezing man's life might depend on the speed with which he could light a fire.

There was another odd thing about Fortymile. It was inside the Canadian border, but it was really an American town. It got its supplies from the United States without customs payments, and the mail was sent out with U.S. stamps. Some of the mines were on Alaskan soil, and the community itself had all the characteristics of the Rocky Mountain mining camps of the American West.

It was from these parent communities that the tradition of the "miners' meeting" was borrowed. Here was an odd example of grassroots democracy that shows the very real difference between the Canadian and the American character and between the Canadian and American legal systems.

The Americans were revolutionaries. They had separated from Europe as the result of a bloody war. They wanted to run all their own affairs from the ground up, and that was especially true on the frontier.

The Canadians, of course, had never known the bloodbath of revolution. More often they preferred to have law and order imposed from above – the North West Mounted Police were a good example – rather than have it spring from the grassroots. That's why the Americans had a "Wild West" and the Canadians didn't.

In the three British Columbia gold rushes, police and courts of justice enforced a single set of laws in the British tradition. The mining law was the same everywhere. The gold commissioner – the man in charge of the camps – had absolute power. The lawlessness that was common in American mining history wasn't known in British Columbia.

In the American mining camps in the Rockies, and later in Alaska, every community had its own customs and its own rules. These were made up on the spot. The miners ran their own community. They held town meetings to dispense justice. Like the placer mining process, these meetings began in California.

The American miners' meeting that operated in the Canadian town of Fortymile had the power of life and death over the members of the community. It could hang a man, give him a divorce, send him to prison, banish him, or lash him. In Alaska all these functions were performed. The Fortymilers at one point hanged at least two Indians for murder.

Under the rules, any prospector could call a meeting simply by posting a notice. An elected chairman acted as judge, and the entire meeting acted as jury. Both sides could produce witnesses and state their cases, and anyone who wished could ask a question or make a speech. The verdict was decided by a show of hands. It is doubtful that the democratic process has ever operated at such a grassroots level.

The first saloon served as headquarters for these

meetings. That became a problem. Sometimes when a man called a meeting to seek justice, he found himself fined twenty dollars for daring to call one at all. The money was spent at once on drinks.

Finally one man rebelled. His name was John Jerome Healy, and he was as tough as hardtack. With his cowlick, his Buffalo Bill goatee, and his ramrod figure, he looked the part of the traditional frontiersman. All of his life he had been seeking out the wild places of the Northwest.

Healy had been hunter, trapper, soldier, prospector, whisky-trader, editor, guide, Indian scout, and sheriff. He had run away from home at the age of twelve to join a band of bandits who tried to seize part of Mexico and form a new republic. He was a crony of Sitting Bull, the Sioux medicine man. He had built the most famous of the whisky forts in Canadian territory and ruled it like a feudal baron, carrying on illegal trade in alcohol with the Indians. This was Fort Whoop-Up, behind whose log palisades Healy had fought off the wild wolf-hunters of the prairie who tried to take it over.

In Montana he was known as the hanging sheriff of Chouteau County. He went after rustlers with a zeal that left some people wondering where crime control left off and lawlessness began. Then, with the frontier tamed, the restless and aging Healy headed north, still hungering for the adventure that had driven him all his life.

He followed gold to Juneau, on the Alaska Panhandle. He pushed on to Dyea Inlet at the foot of the Chilkoot.

It was to his trading post that the dying Tom Williams brought the news of the Fortymile strike in the winter of 1886.

Healy saw there was more than one way to get gold out of the Yukon. He went to Chicago, met up with an old Missouri crony, Portus B. Weare, and explained that money could be made in the Alaska trade. These two set up the North American Trading and Transportation Company to break the monopoly of the rival Alaska Commercial Company. They laid plans to establish a series of trading posts along the river and build a fleet of steamboats.

Healy was the boss of Fort Cudahy, the NAT Company's headquarters, just across the Fortymile River from the main town. He was no man to accept quietly the ruling of the miners' meeting, for he had always been a law unto himself. He didn't intend to knuckle under to the miners of this Yukon camp.

He was not popular in Fortymile. He insisted on sending out bills at the end of the month – something Jack McQuesten never did. And so when his hired female servant hauled him before a miners' court, his enemies were waiting for him.

It was an odd case. The young woman had been brought in from the Outside by Healy and his wife. She insisted on staying out late at night, sometimes all night. Healy told her she couldn't go out again to the dances being held in the main town. She disobeyed him and tried to get back into the house, only to find that he had locked her out.

This dictatorial attitude enraged the miners in a town where freedom of action was almost a religion. They decided in favour of the woman and demanded that Healy pay her a year's wages and her full fare back home.

The old frontiersman paid under protest. But he wasn't finished yet. He had an old frontier friend from Whoop-Up days – Superintendent Samuel B. Steele of the North West Mounted Police. Healy asked Steele for protection under the Canadian law by Canadian police.

At about the same time, Bishop Bompas was sending a similar letter to Ottawa. He said the miners "were teaching the Indians to make whisky with demoralizing effect both to the whites and Indians and with much danger in the use of firearms."

That had come about as a result of a shooting over a poker hand. Jim Washburn, known as the meanest man in town, had slashed a card player across the belly and had received a bullet through the hips in return. Fortymile was in danger of becoming the same kind of lawless community that had formed part of the American Wild West.

The two letters from Healy and Bompas ended Fortymile's free and easy existence. In 1894 Inspector Charles Constantine, a thick-set, gruff and honest policeman, became the first lawman to enter the Canadian northland. By 1895 he had a detachment of twenty police under his command. When a miners' meeting was held to take away a claim from a man who hadn't paid wages, Constantine immediately reversed the verdict and abolished the miners' meetings forever. He had been eight years on the force, and was known for his ability in a rough-and-tumble fight. In Fortymile, he called himself "chief magistrate, commander-in-chief, and home and foreign secretary" of the town.

He was so serious about his work that he had three tables in his cabin, each with a different kind of work on it. He moved from one to the other. Constantine's iron hand was felt in various ways. One of his first acts was to stop the dance-hall girls from wearing bloomers instead of dresses. Another was to collect the tax on all locally made hootchinoo. With these edicts some of the freer spirits decided the time had come to move again. Once more civilization had caught them up.

Chapter Six

The rise of Circle City

THE NORTH WEST MOUNTED POLICE had no sooner arrived at Fortymile than another strange community began to spring up farther downstream, this time on Alaskan soil. It was called Circle City, because it was set at the point where the Yukon River crosses the Arctic Circle. And it was founded by Jack McQuesten. (In American mining law, a "city" is the centre of a mining district – not a metropolis.)

For years McQuesten and his partner, Harper, had been grubstaking men to seek out the legendary "Preacher's Creek" – the one in which a missionary had once seen gold by the spoonful. The gold was finally found, not by white men, but by two mixed-bloods – half Russian, half Indian. It lay on the headwaters of Birch Creek, and within a year the region was producing four hundred thousand dollars annually – a sum worth ten times as much in today's values. It was here that Circle City took form.

This was the dreariest section of the Yukon valley. It lay one hundred and seventy miles (270 km) downstream from

Fortymile at the point where the river spills over the Yukon Flats. Here, the hills seem to sicken and die until they decline to a monotonous waste of sand, while the main river, broad as a lake, moves sluggishly in a huge arc across the Arctic Circle for one hundred and eighty miles (290 km). There is no real scenery here in this desolate domain – only hundreds of tiny islands and grey sand bars on which ducks and geese and plover nest by the millions.

Circle City was as drab as its surroundings. A hodge-podge of moss-chinked log cabins lay scattered along the curve of the Yukon River, stitched together by a network of short streets, many of which were little more than rivers of mud in the spring.

The gold claims lay eighty miles (130 km) back from the river. Birch Creek, on which the gold was found, ran parallel to the Yukon before joining it at the southern end of its curve. The trail from the little community to the mines led across a dreadful land of swamp and muskeg and stunted spruce. There was no game here, but in the summer the swamps swarmed with mosquitoes. The insects were so thick they blotted out the sun and sometimes suffocated pack horses by stopping their nostrils. Sometimes they drove men insane.

Here, in this gloomy settlement, Jack McQuesten was king. He owned the most imposing log structure in town – a two-storey trading post from which rose a flag pole. Each year when the Indian women, by custom, tossed every white man in a moose-skin blanket, McQuesten was honoured by being tossed first. Traditionally they let him escape. A mock battle followed. McQuesten landed lightly on his feet, no matter how high he was tossed, and only at the last ceremony in 1896 when he was older and bulkier did he topple onto his back. At that point the Indian women clustered around him murmuring and patting him as a sign of sympathy.

McQuesten's other partners had scattered. Al Mayo was farther down the river at the mouth of Minook Creek – the same area where Ed Schieffelin had once poked about for gold. Harper and Ladue had poled their way up the river, deep into Canadian territory. But McQuesten staked everything he had on the prosperity of Circle City. He lent so much money that by 1894 the miners owed him one hundred thousand dollars.

For McQuesten continued to give unlimited credit. William Ogilvie, the Canadian government surveyor who established the boundary line between Alaska and Canada, once witnessed his credit system in operation.

Into the store came a miner from the creeks. He asked McQuesten how much he owed.

"Seven hundred," said McQuesten.

"Hell, Jack, I've only got five hundred. How am I going to pay you seven hundred with five?"

"Oh, that's all right. Give us your five hundred and we'll credit you and let the rest stand till next clean-up."

"But Jack, I want more stuff, how am I going to get it?"

"Well, we'll let you have it same as you did before."

"But, dammit, Jack, I haven't had a spree yet."

"Well, go and have your little spree; come back with what's left and we'll credit you with it and go on as before."

The miner had his spree. It took everything he had. But McQuesten, without a word, gave him a five-hundred-dollar outfit and carried a debt of twelve hundred dollars against him on the books. That was the way things worked in those pre-gold-rush days.

Indeed, a spree was the high point of social life in Circle City. Every spree was like every other spree. A man on a spree moved from saloon to saloon, swinging a club as a weapon, threatening the bartenders, pouring the liquor himself, treating the house to cigars and hootch, then driving everybody ahead of him to the next saloon where the performance was repeated.

At the height of such a spree, all the miners would line up on two sides of the saloon and throw cordwood at each other from a pile that stood beside the stove. Then someone would jump on the water barrel to make a speech. He'd upset the barrel and finally roll the stove, red-hot, around the floor.

When the party was over, the man who began the spree would hand his poke of gold dust to the saloon-keeper and ask him to take the damages. Such a spree could last for several days. One such bill for damages came to $2,900.

This could have happened nowhere in the world except in Circle City. But here, far from civilization, far from loved ones, far from a man's roots, it was necessary to blow off steam. Everybody understood that.

The only law in the Circle was the law of the miners' meeting. The town, when it opened, had no jail, no courthouse, no lawyers, and no sheriff. But there wasn't a lock or a key in the community.

Circle City had no post office and no mail service, either. A letter could take at least two months and sometimes a year to reach its destination, and might arrive crumpled and smelly and covered with tar and bacon grease.

Circle had no taxes and no banks, except the saloons, which served as banks. The smallest coin in use was a silver dollar. There was no priest, no doctor, no school, no church. But there were men with Oxford degrees who could recite Greek poetry, especially when they were drunk.

Civilized customs were virtually unknown in Circle. A man might easily rise and eat his breakfast at ten in the evening, because the summers were always light and the winters were always dark. It was light at midnight in Circle in the summer. In the winter it was pitch dark at noon.

There was no such thing as a thermometer to measure the winter's fierce cold. Jack McQuesten invented one by putting out a series of bottles of mercury, whisky, kerosene, and an all-purpose patent medicine known as "Perry Davis Painkiller." These froze in ascending order, and that's how the miners knew how cold it was. On cold days even the painkiller froze in the bottles. Then Circle became a ghostly settlement, the smoke rising in pillars to form a shroud that seemed to deaden all sound, except for the howling of the dogs – the wolf-like huskies and the heavy-shouldered malamutes – who dragged sleds out to the mines.

These dogs dominated the town. They were always hungry. They gobbled everything in sight. Leather gloves and harnesses, gun straps and snowshoes, pots of paste, miners' boots and brushes, and even the powdered resin, which they gobbled up as quickly as it was sprinkled on the dance-hall floors.

One man watched a dog eat a dish rag whole for the sake of the grease in it. Another stood helplessly by while a dog rushed into a tent and swallowed a lighted candle, flame and all.

To stop the dogs from eating their precious cakes of soap, the Indians hung the soap from branches of trees. The town's skyline was marked by the silhouettes of log caches built on stilts to keep supplies away from the dogs, whose teeth could tear open a can of salmon as easily as if it were a paper package. Some, indeed, swore the dogs could tell a tin of marmalade from one of bully beef by a glance at the label!

Men crowded into Circle City, claiming they were looking for gold. But actually they came because they were the kind that wished to be left alone. Where else could a man attempt to cut his throat in plain view without anybody trying to stop him?

One did just that. His name was Johnson and he made a bad job of it because he was drunk. The onlookers, seeing

The dogs of Circle City could eat seemingly anything.

that he was failing, patched him up and told him politely that he might try again if he wished. He didn't. Instead, he grew a black beard to hide his scars and ever afterwards was known as Cut-throat Johnson.

If a man's freedom of action got in the way of that of his neighbours, the miners' meetings took hold. The Mounted Police had cleaned up Fortymile, but they had no way of operating on the Alaska side. Once, when a saloon-keeper had seduced a young mixed-blood girl, a meeting decided that he must either marry her or spend a year in jail – even though there was no jail. The miners were quite prepared to build one on the spot, but were spared this labour when the accused decided to get on with the wedding.

The worst crime in Circle City was not murder; it was theft. When one man stole from a cache, his friends sentenced him to hang. When no one could be found to act as a hangman, they changed the sentence to banishment. The culprit was ordered to live by himself twelve miles (19 km) out of town until the steamboat arrived. The miners took up a collection and bought him a tent, stove, and provisions. Then they said goodbye and never saw him or spoke to him again.

The U.S. government considered these meetings lawful. In fact, the verdict of one of them was sent to Washington and confirmed. That was a murder case involving a bartender named Jim Chronister, and the same James Washburn whose shooting affair in Fortymile had so disturbed Bishop Bompas. After killing Washburn in self-defence, Chronister went before a miners' meeting trial and was acquitted in just twenty minutes.

Out of these meetings a Miners' Association was formed, and later the Yukon Order of Pioneers, a fraternal organization whose emblem was the Golden Rule and whose motto was: "Do unto others as you would be done by."

That sounds like a Sunday-school pledge, not the kind one usually associates with hard-bitten miners. But it was born of experience by men who had learned, over the years, how important it was to depend on one another. Each member swore to help every other member if the need arose, and always to spread far and wide the news of a fresh gold discovery.

In the end, Circle City, though four thousand miles (6,400 km) by water from the nearest city, could not escape the influence of civilized life. By 1896, it had a music hall, two theatres, eight dance-halls, and twenty-eight saloons. They called it "the Paris of Alaska." Money was so plentiful that day labourers were paid five times as much as they were Outside, as the northerners called the rest of the world.

In the big new double-decker Grand Opera House, George Snow, half prospector, half showman, who had once starred with the great Shakespearean actor Edwin Booth, produced classical plays and vaudeville acts. Snow's children appeared on stage and picked up nuggets thrown to them by miners hungry for entertainment.

One group of vaudeville performers, sealed in for the winter with only a limited program of acts, was forced to go through the same routines nightly for seven months, until the audience howled as loudly as the malamutes that bayed to the cold moon.

As the gold flowed into town, the community grew richer. Miners roared into the bars, flinging down handfuls of nuggets for drink and dancing out the change at a dollar a dance. They kept their hats on and clumped about the floor in their high-top boots. They danced from midnight until dawn, while the violins scraped and the sled dogs howled.

The community grew bigger and bigger. Mixed in with the mud of the rutted streets was a thick porridge of chips and sawdust from the newly erected buildings. By 1896, twelve hundred people were living in Circle. John Healy's NAT Company opened a store in opposition to Jack McQuesten. The Episcopal Church bought land for a hospital. The Chicago *Daily Record* sent a foreign correspondent to the settlement, which now boasted that it was "the largest log town in the world."

Culture arrived. Up from the University of Chicago came Miss Anna Fulcomer to open a government school. The miners established a library. It contained the complete works of such literary giants as Thomas Huxley, Charles Darwin, Thomas Carlyle, and the historian Thomas Babington Macaulay. Here were filed the standard illustrated papers brought in from the Outside. There were chess sets for the members and a morocco-bound Bible as well as an *Encyclopaedia Britannica* and an *International Dictionary.*

In 1896 Circle City had its greatest year. The gold production that season exceeded one million dollars. Lots were selling for two thousand dollars apiece. Who could have believed that before the winter was out, this, the Paris of Alaska, would be a ghost town – the saloons closed and barred, the caches empty and left to rot, the doors of the worthless cabins hanging open to the winds, and scarcely a dog left to howl in the silent streets?

CHAPTER SEVEN

∼

On the eve of the big strike

A S THE WINTER OF '96-'97 WORE ON, strange rumours began to filter down from the upper-river country people. Stories seeped in about an almost unbelievable event on a little stream whose name nobody could properly pronounce.

At first nobody believed them. Sam Bartlett floated into town one day before freeze-up on a raft of logs; but all he told his friends was that Joe Ladue, Harper's old partner, was trying to hoax the country so he might make money from the new town he was laying out at the Klondike's mouth.

The town, of course, was Dawson City. It was Ladue who had sent the early prospectors into the Klondike area. Now that they had found what they were seeking, he intended to profit – not from gold but from real estate.

Into Oscar Ashby's smoky saloon, ten days before Christmas, 1896, came two traders with a bundle of mail and some gold from a creek named Eldorado in the Klondike valley – a creek that nobody had heard of.

Ashby read one of the letters to a group of seventy-five sceptical miners.

"This is one of the richest strikes in the world," the letter read. "It is a real world-beater. I can't tell how much gold we are getting to the pan. I never saw or heard the like of such a thing in my life. I myself saw one hundred and fifty dollars panned out of one pan of dirt and I think they are getting as high as a thousand...."

The crowd had heard this kind of talk before. Prospectors are notorious for tall tales. The men laughed, ordered drinks, and forgot about it.

But two old-time sourdoughs, Harry Spencer and Frank Densmore, got a second letter from their partner, a Forty-mile saloon-keeper named Bill McPhee. Densmore was nobody's fool. He fitted up a dog-team and headed upriver to see what was what.

Densmore, who had been fourteen years in the country, had tramped over most of Alaska and was well respected. When he sent back word that the Klondike was really as reported, every man knew that something extraordinary had happened.

By this time, more news had arrived. In January, Arthur Treadwell Walden, a well-known dog driver, walked into Harry Ash's saloon, threw a bundle of letters on the bar, and asked for a cup of hot beef-tea. (No dog driver would be foolish enough to drink whisky in the cold weather; drowsiness could lead to death on the trail.)

Ash paid no attention but began to riffle feverishly

through the mail. He was as much a prospector as a saloon-keeper – a veteran of the stampede to the Black Hills country of South Dakota. For some time he had sensed that something unusual was afoot. At last he found the letter he had been looking for, tore it open, and devoured it, his ruddy face alive with excitement.

"Boys," he shouted, "help yourself to the whole shooting match. I'm off to the Klondike."

An orgy followed as men smashed the necks off bottles and drained the contents. Others rushed about Circle trying to buy dogs at any price. Their value leaped from the going rate of twenty-five or fifty dollars to two hundred and fifty, and then, as they became scarce, to fifteen hundred.

But cabins valued at five hundred dollars were now worthless as the town was emptied. Only Jack McQuesten stayed behind to look after the handful of miners who continued to work the Birch Creek claims.

All that winter and spring, the residents of Circle straggled up the frozen Yukon in twos and threes, the wealthier men racing behind dog teams, the poorer dragging their sleds by hand. All of Alaska, it seemed, was moving toward the Klondike.

One of these would soon be famous. He was a former Texas marshal, twenty-six years old, who had been one year in the country. His name was George Lewis Rickard, but his friends called him Tex. He and his partner pulled a sledload of provisions up the humpy ice of the Yukon, reached the Klondike in twenty-six days, and proceeded to get rich. They bought a half interest in a claim on Bonanza Creek in the Klondike valley, and sold it almost at once for twenty thousand dollars. They bought a piece of another claim and sold that for thirty thousand.

That was the start of a career that made Tex Rickard the most famous boxing promoter of his day. For it was he who was responsible for the success of the greatest sports palace of that time – Madison Square Garden in New York City.

In the procession up the river that winter were two middle-aged women: a Mrs. Adams, a dressmaker, who would shortly be making thirty dollars a day with her needle, and a Mrs. Willis, an energetic laundress.

Mrs. Willis had gone north in 1895 to support an invalid husband, vowing she would never return until she made her fortune. She did just that.

On reaching the Klondike, she staked a claim and began cooking to finance her mining project. She bought a stove, baked bread, and sold it for a dollar a loaf. She needed starch before she could set up as a laundress. Starch was so scarce, a single box cost two hundred and fifty dollars. She cleared that much through the bakery, bought the starch, and set up a laundry. With the proceeds, she paid men to work her claim. She fought off all attempts to jump her claim and, when it began to pay off, refused an offer of a quarter of a million dollars.

Only one member in that ragged procession from Circle

City had no interest in gold and no desire for material wealth. This was the Jesuit missionary, Father William Judge, a one-time apprentice in a Boston planing mill, who for the last dozen years had been a servant of the Lord in Alaska.

His fellow travellers eyed him curiously – a skeletal figure with huge, cavernous eyes behind tiny, gold-rimmed spectacles. He was ill-fed, for he had loaded his sled with medicine and drugs instead of food, and he trudged along in harness with a single dog to preserve the animal's strength.

Judge knew that the new camp, built on a heaving swamp, would soon be facing plague when summer ended. He was determined to build a hospital in Dawson as quickly as possible. He succeeded, but died of tuberculosis before the stampede ended. They called him "The Saint of Dawson."

All that spring, until the ice broke, the ragged procession made its way up the river. In the end Jack McQuesten joined it, for there was nothing left for him at Circle City. Fortymile, too, was an empty ghost town. Both of these two weird little log villages on the banks of the Yukon had simply provided the prologue to the great drama of the Klondike Gold Rush. Except for a few rotting cabins, there is little now left on these sites to remind the visitor of what they represented.

McQuesten was too late to stake the richest ground in

the Klondike, but he managed to secure a small-paying claim that paid him about ten thousand dollars' profit. For him that was enough. After all, it was the largest sum of money he had ever known.

INDEX